First edition published September, 2009
Second edition November, 2009
Third edition January, 2010

Published by Power to Change, Langley, British Columbia, Canada.
www.powertochange.org

Reprinted by permission. *Soul Cravings*, Erwin Raphael McManus, copyright © 2006, Thomas Nelson Inc. Nashville, Tennessee. All rights reserved.

Unless otherwise noted, Scripture quotations are taken from the New International Version of the Bible. Copyright © 1973, 1978, 1984 by the International Bible Society. Used by permission of Zondervan. All rights reserved.

ISBN # 978-1-894605-67-0

Printed in Canada

SOUL CRAVINGS

AN EXPLORATION OF THE HUMAN SPIRIT

ERWIN RAPHAEL McMANUS

PREQUEL

Start a Conversation
icravechange.com

In *Soul Cravings Prequel* Erwin McManus talks about the things our souls long for – destiny, intimacy and meaning. These are huge issues to grapple with and it can help to talk these ideas through. Throughout the book you'll notice several questions. You can use these to start a discussion with friends or go to icravechange.com to talk to a mentor.

It's not always easy to take our hardest questions to the ones we love. If you're looking for someone to talk to, we have email mentors ready to talk right now. Mentors are trained volunteers. They can answer questions, point you to other resources or just listen when you have something to say. Mentors are available any time, from anywhere in the world. Your conversation is confidential, free and secure.

Just click the "Talk to a Mentor" button on the top right of the screen, fill out the form and we'll take it from there. Watch your inbox for you mentor's reply.

Go to **icravechange.com** and start the conversation today.

CONTENTS

CRAVE

I WAKE UP EACH MORNING REMINDED THAT ALL I need to face the day is to breathe deeply of fresh air and to find my way to the nearest Starbucks. Well, actually I live in LA, so I really can live without the fresh air (my lungs have finally adapted to the smog). The caffeine, on the other hand, is essential. Each morning demands its Venti skinny "extra hot," wet cappuccino.

Before you condemn me, let me assure you it's not an addiction but an appreciation. I can quit anytime, and so I don't need to. I'm convinced coffee is an acquired taste. The aroma is better than the flavor, not to mention the compelling nature of the effect.

Science is only now discovering the medicinal value of the sacred bean. If all goes well, it will soon be its own food group. I've never been pregnant (my wife volunteered both times), but I do know the power of cravings. Is my relationship to java a problem? No, espresso is a guilty pleasure, and I am grateful for my dealer … um … barista.

There are cravings within me, though, that pull on me like an addiction.

They have always been with me and have even at times tormented me.

They go far deeper than any physical addiction ever could.
Beyond my flesh,

beyond my mind,

  beyond my heart,

    there seems to be a place where my deepest and
      most powerful cravings lie.

      And they do not lie silently.

My soul, it seems, always desires and demands, and no matter how I try to satisfy it, **it always craves more**. No, not more, but something I can't seem to understand.

My soul craves, but for what I don't know.

And there I tell you is at least half my problem. I've tried so many things and done so many things, certain they would satisfy my soul, but they never did.

Most of the time it was worse than leaving me empty. Not only did I find myself unsatisfied, but the craterlike vacuum inside me was now deeper than it was before.

It seems as if I've spent my whole life trying to satisfy this insatiable part of my being.

If you interviewed my soul, it would probably describe me as sadistic or masochistic. My soul would tell you I find some dark pleasure in leaving it unsatisfied. Before you jump to a conclusion, though, you need to hear both sides. It's not like I wanted to starve my soul to death. I never purposely withheld from it what it needed.

If I saw a guy crawling in the desert desperate for water, I would share whatever I had with him. If I knew where the well was, I would point the way. Heck, I'd even drag him there.

How can I be held responsible when my soul doesn't even know what it really needs?

But what if we could know? What if we must know?

We're all struggling to figure ourselves out. We're all afraid to expose our souls to those who might judge us, and at the same time, we desperately need help to guide us on this journey. If we're not careful, we might find ourselves with everything this world has to offer and later find we have lost ourselves in the clutter.

We are all searching for ourselves, trying to understand who we are, hoping that we might discover our unique place in this world. We are all sojourners on a common quest.

Jesus once said that the kingdom of God is within us. Yet most of us don't even bother to explore the possibility that this might be true.

It seems that what he is implying is that we have a better chance of finding God in the universe within us than in the one that surrounds us.

And it is on this path that I invite you to walk with me. I invite you to engage in an exploration of the human spirit, to journey deep inside yourself and search out the mystery of the universe that exists within you.

This is the question I was asked to face years ago when I found myself desperately struggling to understand myself, trying to measure the weight of this one life. There I was, making my personal contribution to the extensive research being done on the meaning of ink blots.

"What do you see?"

Even at twelve I knew this was a trick question.

He wanted to know what I saw so that he could see inside me. It really is a good question, though. Your retina may be necessary for sight, but your soul definitely shapes what you see. My soul was confused and cold and growing calloused, and I was quickly becoming blind to so many things. When your soul is sick, one of the symptoms is blindness. If we are not careful, we will lose the ability to see such things as beauty, truth, or even affection. More importantly, you may close your eyes to what your soul needs you most to see.

IT'S NOT COINCIDENTAL THAT PSYCHOLOGY IS THE study of the soul. *Psych* comes from the Greek word for *soul, breath, life*. It is specifically the study of human conditions outside the physical domain. Is it possible that much of what we call psychosis and neurosis is really about us being soul sick?

What do you see?

If you can answer this question honestly, you'll get a pretty clear look inside yourself. But more than that, you will begin a journey of self-discovery. For this to happen, I would like to invite you into a story. It is the story of all of us.

I would like to guide you on a soul journey and help you discover that which is already there within you. And you'll ask more than simply, *What do I see?* You'll also ask, *What do I hear? What do I feel? What do I find?*

This will be an exploration of the human spirit, and I am absolutely certain that what you will discover will surprise you.

We are all a part of an epic story – a trilogy. Three quests that we all are on: a quest for intimacy, a quest for destiny, and a quest for meaning. Although all of us go through each of these journeys at some point in our lives and all of us carry within us these soul cravings, they are heightened at different times and places on our journeys.

I should mention that this journey does not focus on empirical evidence attempting to prove God. It is about coming to know ourselves. This is a journal of the human story. It is about our story; and by the way if God exists, we should be able to find him there. I don't know how to prove God to you. I can only hope to guide you to a place where you and God might meet.

The following pages reflect a small part of my journey, and I invite you to join me on my search. I've never believed you can or should even try to force God on someone. This book is my gift to you who are on a genuine search for God. I say it is a gift because I know I can't expect you to open your soul if I do not bare my own.

My soul craves.

If yours does, too, then let's travel together for a while.

DESTINY

Destiny Calling

WHETHER IT'S STRIVING FOR SUCCESS OR LONGING FOR significance, whether it's trying to create a better world or become a better person, there is a drive within us all. We are designed with a need to move forward. Without it our lives become only shadows of what they could have been. You can live without pursuing a dream, you can function without passion, but with each passing moment, your soul will become more and more anemic.

Your soul longs to become, and you can try to ignore it, but soon you will find yourself hating your life and despising everyone who refuses to give up on his or her dreams.

And you can't write this off as cultural conditioning. This is not a characteristic that forms in adulthood; this is something that reveals itself from the earliest stages of our lives. No one has to encourage infants to crawl. With every fiber in our being, we are struggling to move. There comes a point where crawling isn't enough. Though we fall over and over again, we fight our way to our feet, and we begin to walk. Walking is great until we can run, and running is great until we can drive, and for some of us, driving is not fast enough—we just have to fly.

Our intrinsic need to become more can be seen from our

earliest dreams and childhood longings. We humans are instinctively ambitious. When we dream, our dreams naturally gravitate toward greatness.

No one ever dreams of becoming an Olympic swimmer who, after years of hard work and personal sacrifice, manages to come in fourth. Can you imagine a ten-year-old swimmer passionately describing to you how she is working toward the Olympic Games and her ambition is to finish just one place short of a medal? The dream that drives her is to know that she is in the same water with the very best in the world.

We were living in Miami, Florida, when I met a Filipino kid named Billy. He was a couple years older than me and ten times cooler. He was popular, edgy, got all the girls, and played the sax. I quickly concluded I needed to play the sax. I signed up for band and for the next two years played third chair in a section of three. No matter how hard I tried, it just wasn't going to happen. I wasn't born to play the sax, but I have always loved music. Years later I picked up a guitar, messed with a piano, and wrote a lot of songs, but there are miles between me and Miles—Davis, that is. I may not have the skills of a world-class musician, but I have the soul of one.

My house looks like a guitar center has been robbed—sound equipment, microphones, keyboards, acoustic guitars, electric guitar, bass guitar, flute, drums, and yes, even a saxophone. While I think it's not an exaggeration to say I have been the unquestioned impetus for my children's love for music, their aspirations are fueled not by me, but by Neal Pert, Geddy Lee, or Lenny Kravitz. For me it was John Lennon and Paul McCartney when I was young, and Bono and Chris Martin since then. There have been a lot of great bands since the Beatles and Rush and Radiohead and Coldplay, but if we're going to dream, if we're going to pursue a standard of greatness, once again the human spirit naturally gravitates toward the extraordinary. We dream of greatness; we dream ambitiously.

As children we assume that greatness is within our grasp. Whatever inspires us, we begin to dream that one day we will be the best. It is only as we lose our childlike innocence that we begin to settle for far less. A part of growing up seems to be acquiescing to mediocrity. It's easy to say that we're just becoming realistic, that it's just a part of growing up. But, in fact, it's just the slow death of our souls. When we stop dreaming, we start dying. For some of us, this has been a slow, painful death. Others are just walking dead. They died a long time ago, and it's nothing less than a freak of nature that they're still breathing.

Is there room for dreams in a grown-up life?
icravechange.com/1

A Crisis of Success

THE LIFE THAT IS MOST POWERFULLY LIVED IS THE ONE that finds passionate urgency fueled by a sense of destiny. We must become. This is both something we need and something we long for.

One of the most quoted proverbs of Solomon is that without vision the people will perish. He also said that hope deferred makes a heart sick. He seems to be telling us that we need to have a dream we are pursuing and at the same time experience enough of that dream to keep us inspired.

We need both to aspire and accomplish. Without a vision for your life, without a sense of purpose, you will begin to die a slow death.

At the same time, if hope seems only an illusion, if you give up on hope, your heart, your soul, will become sick. It is not only essential to keep hope alive; it is hope that keeps us alive.

Hope is the fuel through which we create the future.

When you give up on hope, you become paralyzed in the present and begin to live in the past.

If you are not looking toward the future, you do not have one.

The baby boomer generation seems to have perfected the cultural phenomenon described as midlife crisis. The classic scenario is, you turn forty, and all of a sudden you start reconsidering everything. You begin having this haunting sense that you've wasted your life and will never fulfill your full potential.

Really there are only two scenarios that lead to midlife crisis.

First, you've given all your life to pursue certain goals and dreams. You've sacrificed everything to get there, maybe even your marriage and children. You've placed everything on the altar of success. Now you're nearing forty, and you realize that you have given everything you have and are still going to fall short of your dreams, goals, and ambitions. So you panic. You find yourself in the middle of a life crisis.

The second scenario is exactly like the first, except for one difference. As you turn forty, you realize that you got there; you accomplished everything you set out to do. You were so sure that it would be worth the sacrifice. Even when you left people behind, you told yourself it was necessary for the mission at hand. Stay focused. Don't get distracted. Win at all costs. And there you were a success. You have become the perfect picture of accomplishment without fulfillment.

You have everything, and you are empty. It all came to nothing.

So you find yourself in the midst of crisis wondering if this is all there is, asking yourself, maybe for the first time, *Is there anything worth living for?*

Sometimes this crisis is solved by moving from success to significance. We've outgrown success. Now we know it's not about that. We've grown up. We just want to be significant. We want to make a difference, to make our lives count. We hope it's not too late. Every day we move just a bit closer to death and a lot farther from birth.

So we redefine our values, reorganize our priorities, and once again begin our search for a future.

Though we have a new compass, we are still essentially on the same journey, trying to become something worth remembering, trying to be someone worth admiring, trying, oh, so desperately trying, to become someone. We are strange creatures, we humans. We strive for success, search for significance, look for purpose, and dream of our destiny.

Why do we need it? Shouldn't we be able to live without it?

The Secret Longing of the Soul

ALL OF US HAVE A DEEPLY ROOTED LONGING NOT only for our lives to be different but to make a difference in the lives of others.

We are created with a need to have hope and to give it.

When we become jaded, we ignore the voice to catch those who are falling over the edge, but it is still there within us and it haunts us. And even when we know something should be done, we just hope someone will do it.

Yes, it is possible to deaden your soul, but not to silence it. The farther we move from God, the more likely we are to actually give up on progress. A superficial assessment would lead you to conclude the exact opposite, given religion is often the enemy of progress, but God never is. When we stop believing the world can become a better place, when we stop caring about the lives and conditions of others, we lose a part of ourselves.

Have you ever stopped caring for the people around you? *icravechange.com/2*

God created us for progress. His intention for us was always that we would be conduits of good. We can insulate ourselves from the problems of the world, but in doing so, we become less than human. When we give ourselves to create a better future, when we choose to become instruments of change, when we refuse to accept the status quo and commit to make the world a better place, something resonates within us. It is beyond reason. It is something far deeper than that. Somehow we know that this is right. It satisfies something deep within you. It's as if your soul has been craving and you didn't know for what. And there it was. Your soul was starving for hope—not just to have it, but to give it.

This is the mystery of the human spirit, that God never intended for us to live hopeless lives. When we treat the future as something that happens to us, we become passive, apathetic, and even paralyzed.

When we embrace our unique place in creation, when we believe that God has created us to create, it begins to change everything for us. It not only empowers us to live, but it holds us responsible for life. Not only our lives, but the lives of everyone we could affect for good.

To live an aimless life is to live an unfulfilling life. You're just not wired to give up on life. The best evidence that your soul craves a destiny is that when you no longer believe you were created with a purpose and for a purpose, your soul is never satisfied with the life you have. You can't get enough, make enough, or buy enough to pay it off. Your misery owns you.

To go beyond feeling, to go beyond compassion, you have to believe that it is right to act, that you were created to bring change. If Jesus was nothing else, he was an activist for change. To be a follower of Christ is to believe that everyone's life can be different. No one is defined by the status of birth. Our destiny is not limited to our pedigree. Every human being is of equal value to God. No one must remain a prisoner of fate.

INTIMACY

Love Is Like Stepping on Broken Glass

ONE BEAUTIFUL CAROLINA NIGHT DURING MY SENIOR year at the University of North Carolina, a group of us decided to escape the dorm and walk to Franklin Street, the mainstay of Carolina life. It was a time for catching up with old friends and making new ones. After getting some food, we all headed back to Avery dorm, and then the most unexpected thing happened. In the midst of a lot of talking and laughing, suddenly there was a loud sound of pain. The person I knew least, but frankly was at-tracted to most, had begun walking barefooted, and she stepped on a piece of glass.

It was impossible for her to take another step.

Everyone was concerned, and every guy wanted to help, but fate seemed to lean my direction. I was the only one who could pick her up and carry her. Thank God for hanging out with a bunch of geeks. I picked her up and carried her for what must have been nearly a mile back to the dorm, all downhill, or at least that's how it seemed. It was magic. She was really light, I was really strong, or I was highly motivated.

And like the plot of a classic novel, a romance was born— the kind you only read about and read with envy. You know, true love, an epic romance, classic Shakespeare. I believe it was Christopher Marlowe who said, "Come live with me and be my Love, / And we will all the pleasures prove." This had to be what was spoken of when the expression "true love" was coined—the kind that lasts forever; the stuff of which poets write for a hundred years.

It lasted a couple of months.

This brings me to the problem with love. It woos you in like a lamb headed toward the slaughter. It steals your heart with promises that seem almost too good to be true, and then you discover that was exactly right.

Perhaps John Donne said it best: "I am two fools, I know, / For loving and for saying so." There's probably no subject ever discussed among human beings that is more captivating and more elusive than love. From Aphrodite to Oprah Winfrey, we look to our mavens to guide us through this tumultuous jungle of human emotions. Every generation writes about love. From *Pride and Prejudice*, the Jane Austen novel, to *Pride and Prejudice*, the British miniseries, to *Pride and Prejudice*, the Hollywood movie, to *Bridget Jones's Diary* (aka *Pride and Prejudice* for those that don't know they like *Pride and Prejudice*), we never seem able to escape the maddening effects of love.

We are driven *by* love, driven *to* love, and even driven *from* love.

Without love there wouldn't be much to sing about, and even music seems torn when it comes to love. Some sing of love as the one compelling reason to live. From the Foo Fighters' "Everlong" to James Blunt's haunting "You're Beautiful," they describe the all-consuming power of love. At the same time you have songs like Aqualung's "Breaking My Heart" and Death Cab for Cutie's "Someday You Will Be Loved" to the old school classic "What's Love Got to Do with It" (Tina Turner for the too-young-to-know), which remind us that there may be no more dangerous place to be than in love.

> How is it that the same thing that can make your life a
>   rhapsody can also leave you gutted,
>   like a dead fish wrapped in day-old newspaper?

Has love ever left you gutted? *icravechange.com/3*

What Must I Do to Be Loved?

WE SPEAK OF TRUE LOVE NOT ONLY LASTING A LIFETIME, but lasting forever. Forever seems to have a clear beginning and end. In the end we can't manage to meet the standards of love, and so we just accept that love isn't all it's made out to be. Prepare to be disappointed. Isn't that the history of love? We can never live up to its standards. I think we recognize this when it comes to God. If God loves conditionally, we're all in trouble. And this, when you whittle it down to its bottom line, is the basis of all religion.

God loves but on condition. Meet the conditions and gain the love. Love is something that is attained. Oh, we use different words for it—*forgiveness, mercy, acceptance, grace*—all really different words for love.

In this it appears that all religions are the same. They give God a name and then establish the rules that we must follow if we are to gain his favor and affection. I think this is why a lot of us see all religions as different ways of getting to the same thing.

Some girls want flowers; others, chocolates; others, meaningful conversation (and you thought the flowers and chocolates were expensive); all different ways of trying to get to the same place—to be loved, to find love. So some people pray five times a day facing east; still others bring offerings, light candles, and memorize incantations; all for the same purpose—to gain acceptance from their Creator.

Really it's absurd to think that any religion would somehow get you to God.

It's like being in love with a person who has no interest in you. He loves your advances only because they make him feel self-important, but really he has no motivation to pursue you. It's all one-sided. He loves being pursued, and so your desire only inspires him to be more elusive. You have to admit, if the premise of religion is valid—if you do this, then God will accept you—this is a more accurate description of God: He's just some really good-looking, smug, and arrogant Divine Being who loves being the object of all our affection.

When it relates to God, we call this one-sided love, which has, over time, become contextualized as an experience, worship.

If you thought about it long enough, it would really make you sick. If you had a friend or anyone you cared about in that kind of one-sided relationship, you would do everything in your power to convince her to dump him. But we want so much to be loved that we allow ourselves to be coerced and demeaned just by the possibility of one day being loved.

I'm often accused of being irreligious, and I suppose it's for this very reason. Whether it's Christianity, Islam, Buddhism, Catholicism, Hinduism, Judaism, or any other *ism*, when a religion is created on the subtle premise that God withholds his love and you must submit to the system to earn that love, I consider it the worst of corruptions.

But again these traps work only because of two things: we long for love, and we are convinced that all love is conditional.

Ironically, this is where so many have a problem with Jesus. For centuries the church has been telling us if we want God to love us, we need to follow the rules. It's been far more important to focus on the sin problem than the love problem. This is the only way the institution can maintain control over our lives. After all, if love is unconditional, what will keep them following our rules? Don't we want people, first and foremost, to be good? If our goal is to get people to conform, you can accomplish that without love, but you can't maintain a civilization without the rule of law.

What governments have not always been able to do, religions have accomplished with amazing effectiveness. They keep people in line.

What in the world would happen if people actually began

discovering the actual message of Jesus Christ—that love is uncon-ditional? What would happen if we began to realize that God was not, in fact, waiting for us to earn his love, but that he was passion-ately pursuing us with his love? What would happen if the word got out that Jesus was offering his love freely and without condition?

Would anyone actually choose to be a slave to ritual and legalism when he could have relationship and love? The answer, unfortunately, is yes. The reason religion works is that we believe in conditional love and doubt the existence of unconditional love.

I have no doubt that there are many of us who have run into religious leaders, church leaders, those who would speak on behalf of God and have held God hostage. It was our responsi-bility to raise the ransom to release his love. There are way too many people being duped into believing that if they give enough money, they will unlock and receive all that God has been with-holding from them.

Some of us have come to our senses and realized we've been taken.

Whatever kind of love you can purchase, it isn't the love your soul longs for. If you have to buy love, it's not even worth the price. I know that many of us look to Matthew, Mark, Luke, and John for our spiritual wisdom, but in this case John, Paul, George, and Ringo got it right—*can't buy me love.*

So again we're face-to-face with a dilemma—we can't earn love, we can't buy love, and we can't live without it.

We know in the pit of our stomachs that if love is condi-tional, it can't really be love at all. We also know that if love is unconditional, we are neither the sources nor the instigators of such love, which again is a part of our conflict. We want what we do not give. We long for what we seem incapable of producing.

Where does the concept of unconditional love come from anyway? How can we hold such a lofty ideal when we live so far from it? Doesn't believing in unconditional love pretty much fall into the same category as believing in aliens from outer space?

Maybe the fact that we love even the most meaningless of things tells us more about our capacity to love than we think.

What we have described as love has become something so superficial, something so thin and without substance, that pretty much anything qualifies as love. If we really knew love, if we knew deep, profound, unending love, maybe we wouldn't love chocolate. While I'm sure God appreciates all these things (after all, he is the Creator of all that is good and perfect), creation is not the object of his affection. When it comes to love, you exist in a unique category. There are a lot of things that are dispensable to God. He can re-create whatever he wants. You, however, are not on that list. You are unique and irreplaceable.

You are the object of God's love.

Do you believe that God loves you unconditionally?
icravechange.com/4

Chased by Love
(Please Don't Run Too Fast)

IN *CHASING DAYLIGHT*, I DESCRIBE A TIME WHEN A TEAM of us were in the Middle East. I had been invited to speak to a group of Muslims, specifically about the history of Christianity. Pressed by my translator to answer a question that I had somewhat evaded, I was left with nowhere to go but to talk more specifically and personally about Jesus. I had been describing to them my own sense of disappointment with and even disdain of the religion of Christianity. They all quickly agreed that as a religion, there were deep problems and inconsistencies between beliefs and practices.

But eventually they wanted to know what exactly was the meaning behind the coming of Jesus. Somewhat apprehensively I began my best effort to translate back into a Middle Eastern context the story of Jesus (after all, this was Jesus' home turf) and, more specifically, why it would be necessary for God to become human. This, from my vantage point, was the story of God. It's a love story, by the way.

"I once met a girl named Kim."

My translator looked at me confused. I'm sure he was wracking his brain, trying to remember some biblical character named Kim. He stopped translating and just looked at me. I encouraged him to simply translate.

"I once met a girl named Kim, and I fell in love."

I continued, *"I pursued her with my love and pursued her with my love until I felt my love had captured her heart. So I asked her to be my wife, and she said no."* I could feel their empathy, if not their pity.

"I was unrelenting and asked her again, pursuing her with my love, and I pursued her with my love until she said yes."

There was huge relief throughout the entire room.

I went on, *"I did not send my brother, nor did I send a friend. For in issues of love, you must go yourself.*

This is the story of God: he pursues you with his love and pursues you with his love, and you have perhaps not said yes. And even if you reject his love, he pursues you ever still. It was not enough to send an angel or a prophet or any other, for in issues of love, you must go yourself. And so God has come.

This is the story of Jesus, that God has walked among us and he pursues us with his love. He is very familiar with rejection but is undeterred. And he is here even now, still pursuing you with his love."

The images we often receive of Muslims are that they're angry, hostile, and violent people. I can tell you that in this moment I knew there was something transcendent that connected all of our hearts and souls together. A belief that was supposed to divide us strangely united us, and I feel most certain that I know why. Every human being longs for love. The possibility that God is love is an almost overwhelming prospect.

In that moment the story of Jesus was not about who is right and who is wrong, what God's name is and who his prophet is, but what exactly God's motivation toward humanity is. If the message that God wants to get across to us is just about getting our beliefs right, then he didn't need to come himself. If God's entire intent was to clarify right from wrong, no personal visitation was necessary. If the ultimate end was simply to overwhelm us with the miraculous so that we would finally believe, then even God's taking on flesh and blood and walking among us were far from necessary.

There is only one reason for God to come himself, because in issues of love, you just can't have someone else stand in for you.

When it comes to love, it has to be face-to-face. There has to be contact. Love cannot exist where there is only distance. Love can survive distance, but only by the strength of what comes through intimacy.

Like Solomon's lover, God is going up and down the streets of the city, traveling the most obscure paths and untamed wilderness, walking on unnamed roads in the most desolate of places, searching for the one he loves—and that one is you and me and every human being who has ever walked this earth, has taken a breath, and has longed for love.

Religion exists not because God loves too little, but because we need love so much. In the end all religions misrepresent God. They either dictate requirements for love or simply become a requiem for love. I think many of us have rightly given up on God on this basis alone. We've been told that God is a reluctant lover and that his standards must be met before there can be any talk of love. This is lunacy. Love exists because God is love. Our souls will never find satisfaction until our hearts have found this love that we so desperately yearn for.

God is not passive, for love is never passive, but always passionate; and passion always leads to action.

Do you see God as a reluctant lover? *icravechange.com/5*

SOUL CRAVINGS

God and Basketball

LOVE CAN NEVER BE SIMPLY BETWEEN YOU AND GOD. It can never be limited to that relationship. Jesus makes that clear. Love is more than the relationship between a man and a woman, no matter how extraordinary it may be. Love is ever expanding. Love always grows, not just deeper, but wider. Love always loves people more and always loves more people. Love calls us to community; love calls us to humanity; love calls us to each other.

When we belong to God, we belong to each other.

There are no outsiders. All outcasts are welcome. If it isn't enough of a gift to receive God's endless and unconditional love, it even gets better than that—he gives us each other.

Our belonging to each other is not incidental, but absolutely essential. It was no one less than Jesus who said the proof of God is found in our love for one another. Where there is no love, there is no God. At the same time, if there were no God, there would be no love.

Jesus is telling us that without love, without genuine belonging, without the power of authentic community, no one should believe that we have come to know God. This might be exactly why you have been hesitant to trust your heart to Jesus Christ. You've been to church, you've been around Christians, and you've been hurt by both. You've created all these intellectual arguments to justify your unbelief, but in the end, you've just been burned. Your conclusions may be wrong, but your instincts are right.

If God is at the core of something, if he exists at the hot, flaming center, what you're going to find is love. Jesus knew this all too well. He warned us against the trappings of hypocrisy. When those who claim to represent him are unloving, those searching for God might conclude he is as well. The problem, of course, is that we are all hypocrites in transition. I am not who I want to be, but I am on the journey there, and thankfully I am not whom I used to be.

A healthy community is not a place of perfect people.

That place just doesn't exist. We all are flawed. If there was a perfect community, it would be ruined the moment I joined it. And it's easier to be patient with people when you realize they're being patient with you. When we don't come clean up front, it creates an unhealthy environment that leads to pretension and hypocrisy.

Strangely enough, the best opportunity for building meaningful relationships is admitting up front that you're not perfect and that you've got issues. Honesty is the only context in which intimacy can develop. For either of these to have a chance, there has to be trust. Love, no matter how you come at it, is a huge risk.

It makes it easier for me to remember that God will never reject me because I'm not good enough and that any community that has His heart will embrace me as I am. Jesus invites us into a community where imperfect people can find acceptance, love, forgiveness, and a new beginning.

Eventually, though, this will require you to have to take the chance and see if God can really love you through people.

We were playing basketball in the backyard, and after we were good and exhausted, I sat down with a guy named Ben, who still had some serious questions about God. Most of our conversation revolved around whether Jesus is God or not. He was more than willing to embrace Jesus as a great teacher, philosopher, or even spiritual guru. His real hang-up was the divinity thing. After a while it hit me.

I just stopped everything I had been trying to do and said, "You're afraid God's going to burn you."

He looked at me and said without hesitation, "Yes, that's exactly right." He went on to acknowledge that pain and baggage from his past definitely factored in to his present doubts.

We're all like that. Jesus knew this. When others hurt us, it becomes a reflection on God. If we risk entering a community that claims access to God and we find ourselves betrayed in the process, it becomes the fastest way to become a practical atheist. If religion can bring us to God, it can certainly take us from him. I can only hope that Ben, as he shares life with our community, will experience the presence of God through the love we have for each other and for him.

Love Is Not a Four-Letter Word

LOVE IS ALL YOU NEED.
GOD Is Love.

Has God ever disappointed you? *icravechange.com/6*

MEANING

The Answer Is the Question (or the Other Way Around)

THERE IS PROOF OF GOD IN ALL THIS, BUT WE'VE BEEN looking in the wrong place. Before you can find God in the answers, you have to find him in the questions.

Maybe the answers come from us, so we come up with a million of them. But the questions . . . there's something mysterious about the questions.

We all ask them;
we all have them;
and no matter where we come from
or what time in history we have lived,
the questions are always the same.
As important as the answers might be,
what's even more revealing is that we even have
questions: ??
Why do we need to know?
What drives us to search for answers?
Where does the "ask" come from?
Every one of us is on a search for meaning.
We are all on a quest (ion).

The arrow that points the way looks not like this: ⟶ but like this: ?

All of us, no matter what conclusions we've come to, are driven by the same thing—we have to make sense of life.

Everything we experience, everything we learn, every bit of information we process, is being integrated by our brains, and we will not have peace of mind until we create some kind of cohesion.

Whatever your view of the Bible may be, whether you believe it is divinely inspired or the product of human effort, you would have to at least acknowledge that it, like all other religious texts, is a part of the grand story of humanity searching for meaning.

Every world religion, every philosophy, every belief system—from anthropology to astrology to sociology to psychology to mythology to science itself—is trying to propose a cohesive view of reality. They're all trying to make sense of life. We're all trying to figure out who we are, why we're here, what this whole thing is about.

If you're sophisticated, you can see the flaws and fallacies of so many different belief systems. You might even look down with condescension at those who believe what you would consider simplistic answers to the complex problems in the world. We once were convinced that the world was flat; that if we danced, the rain would come; that the stars determined our fate in life.

We have outgrown so many fairy tales that we once believed were reality. Maybe it's an inherent flaw in the human species, but we are all predisposed to believe. We'll believe in just about anything.

While we may be able to systematically eliminate everything we believe that later we discover isn't real, we can't escape the very thing that's right in front of us. Every one of us, regardless of race or language or education or generation, regardless of all the variables possible to make us different, is still inclined to believe in something.

While we may disagree on what we believe in and we may argue violently about what is true, what we can't escape is that we are all on the same quest and our soul craving is to find something we can believe in.

The Truth Is, It's About Trust

THE WORLD WILL GET BETTER WHEN WE GET BETTER. With all the progress that we've made since the Enlightenment, we've got to be honest with ourselves and admit that we're not getting better, which is one reason we're quickly losing our confidence in science. There was a time when science was our promise of a better world. We would outgrow our worst primal instincts. This, in part, was the hope of the Enlightenment, that we would educate and elevate ourselves out of violence.

We were the masters of progress, and one day we would no longer hate each other, abuse the powerless, instigate wars, or in any way be inhumane. Science was a promise of progress. We had outgrown God. We no longer needed him to make us good. We could not only be good without God, but through our achievements, we could actually make ourselves better.

Then there were Hiroshima and Nagasaki. Even if we found ourselves standing on the winning side, something in our gut told us that we were all losers in this. Science wasn't creating a better world for us, but a more dangerous one. It seems as if we can improve on everything except ourselves.

If science and God are enemies, how come we tend to blame God even for what science corrupts?

Even Einstein acknowledged the problem was within us: "The release of atom power has changed everything except our way of thinking. The solution to this problem lies in the heart of mankind. If only I had known, I should have become a watchmaker."

In other words, it is better to keep us stupid if we can't become good. The less technology we have, the less damage we can do.

It was in the middle of the last century when we knew that all the technology in the world would not create for us the paradise that had been lost. Maybe it was right to conclude that we can't trust religion or philosophy or history or government or institutions, but what we know for certain is that we can't trust science, and all for the same reason. They're all connected to people, which brings us to the inseparable relationship between truth and trust.

When I was a philosophy student in college, I was struck by how every writer and each belief system had something within it that was compelling. Yet it eventually became clear that every system of thought had gaping holes and shortcomings. Even before I became a follower of Jesus Christ, even when I considered myself a Socratic, I could see that in the end it all comes down to faith. I found myself moving from one view to another and then to another. And I had all the passion of youth to back it up. After a while I began to see beliefs as fluid, interchangeable, and disposable. I couldn't help wondering if Locke or

Hume or Rousseau really knew any better than I did. They were clearly smarter than I am, but I felt certain that behind closed doors, they were just as uncertain.

We were all wanderers in the same forest trying to find a fresh trail to truth.

Some believed God was down the road ahead. Others were convinced it was all a dead end. Maybe we had nothing in common except that we were all lost and trying to find our way. It's hard to be the guide when you don't know where you're going.

In the midst of all this uncertainty, we made a shift from looking for the answers to looking at the questions—which is why I liked Socrates so much (not to mention that he was willing to die for his convictions).

Even when we don't know what is ultimately true, most of us would follow someone whom we absolutely trust.

Accuracy is less important to us than authenticity.

If no one knows the answer, does anyone know the way?

I began looking for truth in an entirely new way. I was no longer looking for the best idea but the best life. Whatever I would come to believe in, it could not simply change my mind; it had to change my life.

Was any truth out there not simply worth believing in but becoming it? What does an idea look like when it is fleshed out? That's where Jesus came into the picture. His words were straight to the point. His was more than a claim to know the truth; He claimed that he was the truth. The implication of this claim is huge. Is it possible that truth is more than an idea and that it is found in God? What Jesus is telling us is that truth exists in God and comes from God.

When we search for truth, we search for God. Our souls crave the One who is true.

Truth does not exist in a vacuum. Truth exists because God can be trusted. When our souls drive us to search for truth, we are actually longing for God. It's easier just to trust in myself. If you think it's easy to believe in God, you can't even begin to imagine how hard it is to put your trust in him. I had moved from searching for a system of beliefs to searching for someone I could believe in. Somehow I had moved from truth to trust.

This is at the core of our search for meaning.

Can trust be more important than the truth?
icravechange.com/7

It's Not Supposed to Make You Sick

WHAT'S SO FRUSTRATING IS THAT SO MANY THINGS that have the name of Jesus on the label have nothing to do with Jesus in the end. This is a real problem when we are trying to make sense of life. Most people I meet, whenever they learn of Jesus, are deeply drawn to him, yet many of them keep themselves at a distance from Jesus all the same. It doesn't take long to realize that what restrains them from trusting in Jesus is not the compelling nature of Hinduism or humanism or Buddhism or even atheism. The real obstacle that most people struggle with when it comes to Jesus is this thing called Christianity. I've never been a real fan of religion anyway. Once during a series of lectures at Borders in West LA (near UCLA), a very kind and compassionate woman told me that I shouldn't be so hard on religion, that it was a great halfstep in a person's journey toward God. I told her that my experience was exactly the opposite.

Usually religion is a halfstep away from God.

Another time a self-proclaimed atheist e-mailed me the most surprising letter. He sent me a passionate argument for the value of religion. He accused me of being too hard on religions in general and advocated their value as a psychological catharsis. I e-mailed back that I found myself in a surprising place in my relationship with him. He was a religious atheist, and I was an irreligious pastor. I tried to explain to him as a follower of Jesus Christ that I felt it was important to expose and oppose corruption anywhere I found it, whether it was in Islam or in the U.S. government, whether it was in Catholicism or in evangelical Christianity.

Whenever religion is used to manipulate or control people, I consider it the enemy of humanity and the enemy of God.

I just don't have a lot of patience for people who use the name of God to try to control people through guilt and shame. If God's love isn't freely given, it's not worth receiving anyway—because then it wouldn't be real. It's a curious thing that Jesus is like a cold drink on a hot summer day, but Christianity can be like spoiled milk.

I took an international team to Damascus, Syria, in the summer of 2000. What an amazing place to travel and experience standing in the middle of one of the oldest cultures in the world, not to mention the capital for global terrorism. We were warned before we entered that choosing to go there was inherently dangerous and could even be life-threatening. To my unfortunate surprise, they were right. The trip almost killed me. In fact, if I remember correctly, three of us were fighting for our lives.

We had been poisoned.

We traced it back to what we thought was the most innocent of things. All three of us drank Diet Coke. The can said "Diet Coke" in big, bold American-like print. It was the fine print that was far more important—"bottled in Syria." We thought we knew what we were getting, but we were tragically mistaken. Some mistakes don't cost you much; this one cost us everything we had, or at least everything we could have. It looked like the real thing, but three of us lived as witnesses that it was a counterfeit.

There are unfortunate similarities between Syrian Diet Coke and Western Christianity. You can't let the name on the label fool you. You're not getting what you think you're getting.

Just because Jesus and his logo are imprinted on the outside of the container doesn't mean that what you're drinking is the real thing. If you find yourself keeled over in agonizing pain, wondering why you're sick to your stomach, it may be that what you got was a counterfeit version of the Christian faith.

It seems almost counterintuitive that there are people who are running hard and fast away from the church and are, at the same time, desperately and earnestly searching for God.

If you stepped into a toxic religious environment, you were right to run, even if Jesus' name was attached to it. And by the way, when you did that, you weren't running farther from Jesus, but closer to him. You just have to be careful not to come to the tragic conclusion that just because you've experienced something that was false and maybe even toxic, there is nothing that is true. Even when you find yourself frustrated, even when you feel that you've been duped or deceived, even when you think something is true and later discover it is false, you should take solace in this: something inside you knows the difference.

Something within you not only compels you to search for truth, but has a soul reaction to it.

Can you connect to God without Religion?
icravechange.com/8

DISCOVER

SOMETIMES I FEEL LIKE MY SOUL IS NOTHING MORE than a leaky faucet. You know, the kind that drips all night long. It's not really a loud sound, but after hours and hours of drip, drip, drip, the sound not only echoes, it begins to intensify. The more silent the room, the louder the sound becomes. Before you know it, it consumes the whole room. You would give anything if you could just shut it off.

After a while, if the water keeps dripping long enough, it moves from deafening to silence. You just can't hear it anymore. It becomes white noise, backdrop. It's still making noise; it's still calling out, but you can't hear it anymore. It goes from thunder to silence and, then when you least expect it, back to thunder.

Soul cravings are like that. They scream in your head until your ears hurt. But after a while, it's a silent scream. You can't hear it anymore, and you could almost deny it completely except for the echo deep within the hollowness of your soul.

You don't know what your soul wants. You can't find what your soul needs, so you lose your soul. You just have to ignore it and go on.

The Foo Fighters put my frustration to music.

All my life I've been searching for something
  Something never comes
    Never leads to nothing
      Nothing satisfies but I'm getting close
        Closer to the prize at the end of the rope.

We can get lost in desires and never find what our souls long for.

Instead of facing the hard reality that what we're pursuing is not what our souls crave, we just try to solve the problem by getting more—more toys, more money, more power, more prestige, more sex, more stuff. We spend our lives trying to satisfy our souls. Some things are only a facade. Some things satisfy for a moment. Some things deaden our souls.

It's kind of weird when you think about it—to gain the whole world and lose our souls.

You are on a journey of the human spirit.

I've been married to Kim for over twenty-two years, and I can tell you she's an ever-expanding universe. The more I get to know her, the deeper I realize she has become. I'll never know her completely, and in fact, she'll never know herself completely because she's not a stagnant being. You can't completely know someone who is always growing, always changing, always expanding. This is what I love most about Kim. She's not the woman I married over twenty years ago. She's far more than that.

I wish I could say that's true for everyone, but I don't know that it is. Some people seem to live in a very small universe. Their world has room only for themselves. While their souls have every potential to be ever expanding, they seem instead to be the center of a collapsing universe— no room for dreams, for hope, for laughter, for love, for others—room only for themselves.

They find themselves very much alone, and they are very lonely. Strangely enough, they don't know why. Their souls crave too. And the way they have gained the whole world and lost their souls is that they have made themselves their whole world. They have sold out.

Most of us don't sell our souls to the devil; we just give them away.

You can play it safe and hide away behind indifference and choose the path of mediocrity. Remember you can swallow almost anything. The question is, can you keep it down? We live in a world filled with indifference, apathy, detachment, conformity, compliance, and acquiescing to the status quo. We swallow, but it doesn't settle well. The human spirit has no appetite for the bland, the mundane, or even the passionless. When you stop believing you are unique, something begins to die inside you.

What is it in the human spirit that insists on its uniqueness? It is not enough for us to simply exist. That every one of us has a unique fingerprint means more to us than simply improvements in forensics. We are nothing less than driven to find our own paths, make our own way, be our own person. While we love to have things in common with others, we desperately need to believe we are in some way unique. We want to be the same as and different from those around us.

We want to have things in common, but we don't want to be common.

We are made up of nothing but ordinary material. Yet something inside us cries out that there is more to us than what meets the eye. We are like a cloth made of burlap and cashmere. We are without question on our way to becoming dust. Is this all it means to be human, or is there more?

Even as you read this, there is a voice coming not from your head but from your gut, screaming that you are more than water and disposable material. So much of your life journey can be explained by your soul cravings. Your soul knows its uniqueness. And a voice somewhere deep inside you longs to discover it. It calls you out and beckons you to pursue it.

There is something out there to be found, and our souls are restless to find it.

All of us begin our lives fueled by curiosity, yet far too many of us replace it with conformity. We are born unique but can die standardized. Henry Ford offered his Model T in any color customers wanted as long as it was black. He was the master of standardization. This wasn't even a sustainable idea for cars, much less for people. We are not supposed to look like or act like and certainly not live like we are the products of an assembly line.

It's way too easy to live our lives by default. If we are not careful, we can become the sum total of all the expectations others impose on our lives. We allow ourselves to become generic, standardized, homogenized. We maintain the status quo. Conform to the expectations of others.

Suppress our curiosity. Stop questioning. Keep from stirring things up. Line up and march in single file. We just get in line, never asking why we're even standing there at all.

My son, Aaron, and I were in London last December. One night we decided to catch a movie over in the Piccadilly Circus area. It was rainy and cold, and there was a long line of people waiting to buy tickets. I didn't want to stand in line and get wet, so I looked for an alternative route. Just to the right of the queue I noticed another window that appeared available with no one waiting in line. I asked the person manning the booth if he was open, and he said yes with a look of surprise on his face. We asked why no one was in his line, which was empty, and everyone chose instead to stand unquestioning in the rain. "I have no idea" was his response. While I was buying our tickets, Aaron felt compelled to free those trapped in the other queue. They were reluctant to believe him.

Why are we more likely to get behind someone in line rather than start our own?

Eventually we find ourselves a part of a human assembly line surrounded by standardization, routine, and predictability. We find ourselves miserable in the mundane. One day we find ourselves looking in the mirror, wondering who we are and why we are. Is life arbitrary, or is there meaning behind it? Am I unique or incidental?

What we are searching for is rooted in where we come from and in who we are.

From your first breath you have been on a journey. There are things your soul longs for, and whether you have yet recognized it or not, your life is shaped by your search for them.

You are on a quest to discover your own uniqueness—who you are, why you are here, and where you are going.

Eric Bryant and I were on our way to Adelaide from Sydney when we finally saw the writing on the wall: not expected, not replaceable, not bland, not usual, not common, not typical, not standard, not humdrum, not parity, not obvious, not predictable, not similar, not comparable. What makes you special?

Unique.

If we find ourselves endlessly thwarted in the search for our uniqueness, we may choose to end our quest and settle for a sterile life of empty existence. We must be careful not to mistake surrender for rest.

We seem destined to be tormented by cravings we cannot satisfy or to live dissatisfied lives dead to our deepest longings.

My earliest memories were longings coming from somewhere deep within me. I didn't have a language for them then, but that doesn't mean they didn't speak to me as forcefully at the age of eight as they have at the ages of twenty-eight and forty-eight.

When I was only a small child, I believed in God, in love, and in laughter. To believe in these things is natural to the human spirit. For a child, more is unknown than known. To believe in God, in mystery, in the unseen, is not difficult for a child. Children are born to believe. They are the perfect candidates for myths and fables and fairy tales. As adults, we see this as a weakness, proof of the naïveté of childhood.

As we grow older, we know better. It's funny how as adults, we struggle with faith. We need evidence to justify our belief in the invisible. We attempt to build faith systems constructed with our logic and reason. As children, we just believed. Faith was so natural. Yes, our innocence left us vulnerable to believing things that are not true, but is it possible that this same innocence exists so that we may find that which is most true? We are created with a natural inclination to believe.

We don't grow *into* faith; we grow *out* of it.

We have within us both the ability and the disposition to look beyond the material and search for the eternal. If God exists and we were created to know him and faith is the means by which that happens, wouldn't it make sense that we would be born with this inclination? For some, to believe in God is way too much of a stretch. They consider it an insult to their intelligence. For them believing in something they cannot see is absurd. And if you talk about the effect of God on people's lives, they will insist that secondary evidence is not enough. It has to be primary, or it's not real.

So then there is love.

Some people who do not believe in God are consistent and don't believe in love either. No primary evidence. In fact, my non-scientific research has found a direct correlation between losing faith in love and losing faith in God. But for many people it is at this point where they simply live with the inconsistency. You can't see God; you can't prove God in the laboratory. Believing in God is a stretch, but they believe in love. But you can't see love. You can't prove love. The only evidence available is secondary. No primary evidence. Yet when you love someone, you are more certain of that than of almost anything else.

Your soul craves truth, beauty, wonder, love. Your soul craves to dream, to imagine, and even simply to understand. Your soul craves to connect, to commune, to create.

And once you are fully convinced all these things are illusions to be dispensed of, your soul becomes sick. When you cannot see the possibility of these things, when you give up on them, when you are no longer changed by the pursuit of what seem to be ideals outside your reach, you starve your soul and you lose yourself.

Solomon once wrote that God has set eternity in the hearts of men, but that in the end we can't seem to make any sense of it. He somehow knew deep within us is our greatest evidence for God and our greatest connection to God. Jesus said the kingdom of God is within, yet for two thousand years after him, we have kept looking outward for this kingdom rather than inside us. I am absolutely convinced of this one thing: God has placed cravings within your soul that will drive you insane or drive you to him. Your soul longs for God; you just may not know it yet.

I lose things all the time. I've spent hours looking for whatever I lost. When I was a kid, I used to think God was punishing me by hiding the missing object. I was sure I committed some heinous crime against God and humanity, and now God was punishing me by hiding my shoes. My mom would be furious. It must have been frustrating to have a son who lost everything.

Losing things drove me to prayer. I would spend every minute of my search begging God to help me find whatever I had lost. I would think of everything I did wrong and try to make it right—make my bed, clean the closet, take all the stuff I'd hidden under the bed, pull it out and put it in the right place. I would scour my mind for anything I possibly could have done wrong and do whatever I could to make it right. I was frantically trying to find the one thing God was holding against me so I could get him to give back what was missing.

You might think this was a ridiculous thought process, but frankly it worked a lot. Most of the time I was able to get God off my back, repair whatever breach in the cosmos I had created, and find the missing pair of shoes or watch or wallet or whatever happened to be lost at the time. Looking back, I realize that the one thing that seemed to be lost all the time was me. I kept looking for me. Or really for who I was.

Somewhere along the way I became lost.

Do you ever wonder how your life ended up here?
icravechange.com/9

We try to fill ourselves with everything we can grab, and yet there remains an inescapable emptiness within. Even when we've looked everywhere else, even when there's nowhere else to look, we still somehow neglect to consider the possibility that what our souls long for is God. We can't take enough or make enough to fill the hollowness within us. No matter what we try or do we can't avoid the void.

Maybe that's what Jesus meant when he said, "What is it worth to gain the whole world, but to lose your soul?" Was he describing someone like you or me? We spend our whole lives as slaves to our desires, determined to somehow satisfy the deepest longings of our souls. We take everything we can get; we keep everything we can grab; we become human versions of a black hole.

The things we choose in our freedom soon hold us as their prisoners. Our passions can create the exhilaration of freedom while leading us straight into a dark and merciless dungeon. Not all free acts lead to freedom. There is also the added dynamic that the very nature of those things that are counted as sin have a corrosive, corrupting, and addictive nature to them. Their very essence will destroy you and most likely damage or hurt those closest to you.

This is why the Bible talks about human experience in terms of being slaves to sin. One of the odd characteristics of sin is that it is a free act that enslaves you. Sin creates the illusion of freedom. In the end it fools us into seeking freedom from God rather than finding freedom in God.

Whatever else Jesus came to do, one thing is clear—He came to set you free. And so earnest is He about your freedom that He was willing to be taken captive and crucified on your behalf just so you could run free. something our souls long for that we cannot fully understand.

Maybe this is why there's something inside us that pulls us toward God. We were created for freedom, and our souls long to be truly free. Doesn't it make sense that if we were created for relationship with the Creator of the universe, he would leverage everything within us so we would search for him, reach out for him, and perhaps even find him?

So we're back to hide-and-seek. You might be asking yourself, If God wants me to find him and my soul craves to do so, why doesn't he make it easier than this?

Have you ever gone searching for God?

I have. Frankly I didn't feel like he was cooperating at all. And when you add my propensity toward losing things, how in the world was I supposed to find God?

When you lose something, you have to backtrack.

So I asked around and I looked for God the last place someone saw him—in religion. After all, millions of people around the world go to see God every week unless, of course, you interview them and you realize they didn't see him either. They were just there looking for him, hoping they could find him. There may be nothing more confusing or frustrating than having tried God and walking away with nothing but the bad taste of religion in your mouth.

My grandmother was Roman Catholic, and so I began my journey in a Latin Mass. I remember seeing that crucifix and feeling very badly for God. It's hard to be mad at God when He's in worse shape than you. I felt great empathy for him. I also felt a huge sense of gratitude to hear that Jesus died for the sins of the world. I knew very little about sin at the time, but from what I heard, it was a real problem. I, on the other hand, had other issues I was trying to resolve. I know it sounds selfish, but I really needed someone who could help me, and God didn't seem available.

I remember once when I was ten, trying to run away from home, getting caught, getting in trouble, getting grounded, sitting in my room, and yelling at God from the top of my lungs. I remember telling God off and then pausing to see what would happen. Nothing happened, and that seemed to be the worst thing that could happen.

So many of us spend our lives worrying that God is going to punish us or hoping that God is going to help us, but neither one of those things ever seems to happen.

For all the activity that there is in the world trying to get God's attention, it can leave you wondering whether it's all just a horrible waste of time. You couldn't really blame God, though. I never really got mad at him or anything like that. I figured he was just way too busy with more important stuff or maybe more important people. So much of my life I felt invisible. It seemed pretty arrogant and presumptuous of me to think God would actually see me. Probably God is only a big picture kind of guy. Maybe he's just not that into details. Or maybe, just maybe, there's more going on than we know.

Over and over again Jesus taught the value of the one to God. He described God as the shepherd who leaves the ninety-nine sheep to find the one that is lost; the woman who searches for the one coin that is missing until she finds it; the father who waits for his wayward son to return home to him.

The one matters to God.

Steven Spielberg explores the theme of the one in several of his films. From *E.T.* to *A.I.* to *Schindler's List* to *Saving Private Ryan*, Spielberg seems almost consumed with the journey of the solitary individual. In *Saving Private Ryan* we find a true story of how a troop of men marched through a world war to find and secure the safe return of one soldier. The movie raises important questions: What is the value of one human being? To what extreme should we go to save one person?

I used to think that I was desperately searching for God. I've changed my mind about that. Looking back, I realize that God was desperately searching for me. I used to wonder why my soul ached and God wouldn't do anything about it. Now I know that it was that very pain that drove me to God. Life without God is starvation of the soul. I thought for a while that God could meet my needs and stop my soul cravings. Now I know that isn't the case.

My soul doesn't crave something from God; my soul craves God. And by the way, so does yours.

That's why everything else will leave you unsatisfied in the end. But don't let this frustrate you; just let it fuel you. All the evidence you need to prove God is waiting within you to be discovered. We have traveled together through these pages, but the journey does not end here. We are at a crossroads but not a dead end. There are decisions to be considered, choices to be made, steps to be taken. You might want to take a moment to turn your head and look back. You have journeyed farther than you know.

If you are still with me, you are very much the kind of person Jesus spoke of in the highest terms. He calls you a seeker and assures you that if you seek, you will find.

He also promises that if you knock, the door will be opened, and if you ask, what you seek will be given to you. He isn't talking about material possessions here as much as meeting the deepest longings of your soul. So continue to seek, knock, ask, and don't stop until you find, enter in, and come to know the answer your soul has been asking all along.

Your soul craves, and it's God you are longing for. So listen carefully to the conversation going on inside your head. Don't worry. You're probably not going crazy. I do know in this case you're not talking to yourself. God is trying to get your attention and bring you into relationship with him. If you will pay attention to your soul, it will guide you to God.

There is more unexplored space within you than there is in this ever-expanding universe.

I am certain that if you will take the time to journey to the depths of your soul, you will not leave there disappointed, and perhaps to your surprise and astonishment you will find God there. I hope these brief entries from *Soul Cravings* have at least helped you start your journey.

Then what will you do?

Have you found yourself face-to-face with God and felt his presence touch your soul like a gentle breeze against your face? How will you respond to him?

To trust in God, you have to know that he loves you without condition. This is the beauty of Jesus' death on the cross. It is God's declaration of love for you. In fact the entire story of Jesus is a story of love that God so passionately loved humanity that he sent his son into human history. Jesus walked among us as the flesh and blood demonstration of love. Jesus is love wrapped up in skin.

His ultimate demonstration of love was his sacrifice on our behalf. You see the death of Jesus Christ, his crucifixion, isn't an incidental act. It's central to who God is and what he's about. He came to demonstrate his love for you and for me because God passionately loves you and me. God is the passionate lover of humanity.

His love embraces you wherever you are on your journey, and he does not leave you there. He launches you on a quest to pursue the life you were created to live. Your soul knows there is a greater purpose for your life, a Godsized dream waiting to unfold and become your future.

We're all on a quest for intimacy, for meaning, for our destiny. Our souls crave love and faith and hope. We are all searching for what our souls long for, and we will be satisfied only in God.

I guess it will never be easy, but Jesus has made it possible. You don't have to be afraid to commit your life to someone who gives his life for you.

Maybe you're different than I am, but I think that we're probably a lot alike in this.

Your soul craves to believe.

You've been burned, maybe you've even been deceived, but deep in your gut, somewhere deep inside, there's a voice telling you that God can be trusted with your life, that you can trust someone like Jesus.

His love is pure and your soul thirsts for him like water is needed by a crusted desert.

Only with God will you have the eyes to see all the beauty, wonder, and opportunity that is around you. Jesus walked among us so that we could get close enough to hear him, to see him, to touch him, to smell him, to know him.

To know him, this is what your soul craves.

Go to **icravechange.com** and start the conversation today.

Discussion Questions:

1. Is there room for dreams in a grown-up life?

2. Have you ever stopped caring for the people around you?

3. Has love ever left you gutted?

4. Do you believe that God loves you unconditionally?

5. Do you think of God as a reluctant lover?

6. Has God ever disappointed you?

7. Can trust be more important than the truth?

8. Can you connect to God without Religion?

9. Do you ever wonder how your life ended up here?

10. Has God been trying to get your attention?

Join the conversation on the blog:
icravechange.com/discuss

If you enjoyed *Soul Cravings Prequel* you'll want to read the complete version, *Soul Cravings*.

The search of your life, is the search for your life.

In *Soul Cravings* Erwin McManus shows readers how our need for intimacy, meaning, and destiny point to the existence of God and our need to connect with Him. This book will deeply stir readers to consider and chase after the spiritual implications of their souls' deepest longings.

Order your copy today at **powertochange.com/store**

CRAVE **MORE?**

 WATCH A SERIES OF VIDEO CLIPS:
icravechange.com/video

 LET US KNOW WHAT YOU THINK:
icravechange.com

 JOIN LIVE CHAT:
icravechange.com/chat

 BECOME A FAN ON FACEBOOK:
icravechange.com/facebook

 FIND US ON YOUTUBE:
youtube.com/icravechange

 FOLLOW US ON TWITTER:
twitter.com/icravechange

Erwin McManus